W9-AOO-600

SPIRITUAL COOKING WITH YAEL

Recipes & Bible Meditations from the Holy Land

WINTERS
PUBLISHING GROUP

YAEL ECKSTEIN

Published by Winters Publishing
2448 E. 81st St.
Suite #4802
Tulsa, OK 74137

Book design copyright © 2014 by Winters Publishing. All rights reserved.
Cover and Interior Design by Stephanie Mora
Illustrations by Katie Brooks

Published in the United States of America

ISBN: 978-1-63185-587-0
        978-1-63185-054-7
Cooking / Regional & Ethnic / Middle Eastern
14.01.30

Table of Contents

INTRODUCTION

I am a mother. I am a wife. I am a professional woman - three unique identities, three very different sets of challenges and responsibilities. Although the roles are different in many ways, they are all expressions of the deepest parts of me, nurtured and sustained by my Jewish faith. The Bible teaches us that even the most mundane tasks can be elevated to a high spiritual level by our thoughts, actions, and intentions. Food is a good example of this. In Judaism, food is regarded as a gift from God. Food is transformed from a purely physical experience to a spiritual event by the blessings we make before and after we eat or drink anything, and recognizing where our sustenance comes from. The act of blessing and drinking wine and challah is the hallmark of the Sabbath and holiday table. In fact, the family table is a central focus in Judaism, a place where tradition is taught and perpetuated. The family table and the experience of eating together is considered to be so essential to Jewish life that the table is compared to the alter in the ancient Holy Temple in Jerusalem.

Cooking three meals a day, day in and day out, can become drudgery. But it is possible to elevate the act of cooking, to imbue it with great significance. It is possible to use cooking as opportunity for meditation, self-reflection, and spiritual growth. If we use the time that we're cooking to pray and reflect, that energy flows into the food that we serve our families and our guests.

In this book, I offer Biblical verses and my interpretations along with recipes. These are verses that help me bridge the gap between the mundane and the spiritual, verses that help me transform the act of cooking into something meaningful and holy. When I focus on Bible verses and mediation while I cook, cooking is no longer a mundane activity that I dread but rather a prime opportunity to develop my inner being. The act of cooking transforms from the purely mundane, into the spiritual.

I have also developed recipes that are simple, healthy and delicious, and that can easily be doubled and tripled to serve more people. I cook for my family daily, and for the many guests we have at our Shabbat table every weekend. By focusing my mind on the purpose of every action, it is easy to find the beauty, and by using these easy and delicious recipes, I can enjoy the preparation as well as the sacred time I spend with my family and my guests.

I invite you to integrate your Bible study and your spiritual life with the very physical act of food preparation. I am certain that, like me, you'll bring renewed energy and enthusiasm to the Godly task of feeding and nurturing your family.

With blessings from the Holy Land,
Yael

"THE VIRTUE OF ANGELS IS THAT THEY CANNOT DETERIORATE; THEIR FLAW IS THAT THEY CANNOT IMPROVE. MAN'S FLAW IS THAT HE CAN DETERIORATE; AND HIS VIRTUE IS THAT HE CAN IMPROVE."

—HASIDIC SAYING—

"GOD DWELLS WHEREVER
MAN LETS HIM IN."

—RABBI OF KOTZK—

Peace be to you, fear not

Genesis 43:23

Fear is an enemy that can prevent us from pursuing our dreams and achieving our goals. We all experience fear of failure, ridicule and disappointment, and that fear can sap our strength, weaken our resolve and steal our ambition. Recognize your dreams and follow them where they lead. Success is born in the pursuit of dreams, and failure only happens when you give up before you try. Open your heart to the universe and let go of your fears. Enjoy the road and be open to a vast array of destinations; trust that the path will take you to the right place.

SALADS
& DIPS

chef salad

CHEF SALAD

I love making this chef salad because it really highlights the beauty of nature that God created. With lots of colors and flavors, this salad looks beautiful on the table and tastes amazing.

INGREDIENTS

3 cups lettuce
2 carrots, shredded
1 cup purple cabbage, chopped
1 avocado, cubed
1 cup cheddar, shredded
¼ cup raisins
2 tablespoons sesame seeds
2 tablespoons sunflower seeds, salted

CREAMY DRESSING

1 cup mayonnaise
½ small onion
2 tablespoons red wine vinegar
½ tablespoon brown sugar
¼ teaspoon garlic powder
salt and pepper to taste

- In a blender or food processor, combine all dressing ingredients.

- Pour over salad immediately before serving.

HUMMUS

Humus is a staple food in Israel which is served at nearly every meal. For breakfast we dip vegetables in Hummus, for lunch we'll eat it on bread, and for dinner it is a side dish. This delicious and healthy dip is surprisingly easy to make, and stays good in the refrigerator for up to a week.

INGREDIENTS

15 ounce can chickpea beans, drained and rinsed
15 ounce can garbanzo beans, drained and rinsed
⅓ cup tahini paste
4 cloves garlic
½ cup fresh lemon juice *or* to taste
1 tablespoon extra virgin olive oil, plus more for garnish
¾ teaspoon cumin
½ teaspoon salt *or* to taste
sweet paprika to decorate

- Place all ingredients in a food processor with the blade insert.

- Pulse for 50 seconds then process until smooth.

- Place the smooth, ready Hummus in a shallow bowl. With a spoon create a small well in the middle, fill the well with olive oil and paprika and serve.

SPEAK TO THE EARTH, AND IT SHALL TEACH THEE

JOB 12:8

The beautiful harmony of the natural world is one to cherish and learn from. The rain falls, the fruits, plants and vegetables grow, animals are fed, human life is sustained. The cycle of Nature is an ecosystem that, when undisturbed, is a chain that provides for all. Take a moment to recognize the journey taken by the water in our cup and the food on our plate and open yourself up to amazement and appreciation. We have the same ability to provide sustenance to others by sharing a nice word, a kind smile or a nutritious meal. Find your way to give life to others!

Cole Slaw

This is one salad that I always have in my fridge. I make the shredded vegetable mix and salad dressing, and then keep them separate until right before I'm ready to eat it. This traditional Jewish salad is simple—yet delicious—and goes great with everything. It tastes wonderful with both meat and dairy meals, or can be eaten as a healthy snack throughout the day.

INGREDIENTS

½ head purple cabbage, shredded
½ head white cabbage, shredded
2 carrots, shredded

- Mix it all together and then dress before serving.

DRESSING

4 tablespoons mayonnaise
2 tablespoons mustard
1 tablespoon sugar
1 tablespoon rice vinegar
1 tablespoon lemon juice
½ teaspoon soy sauce
salt and pepper to taste

Colorful Lettuce

This is a quick salad that I whip up last minute when I have tons of guests coming over and feel nervous that there isn't enough food. This salad takes just a few minutes to prepare and has only a few ingredients, yet it looks and tastes delicious.

Ingredients

4 cups mixed baby lettuce
1 cup purple cabbage, chopped
1 carrot, shredded
1 red pepper, chopped
1 avocado, cubed
½ cup chickpeas from a can, drained

- Mix together all ingredients; pour dressing on to the salad immediately before serving.

Salad Dressing

1½ tablespoons balsamic vinegar
3 tablespoons extra virgin olive oil
1 teaspoon honey
1 teaspoon dijon mustard
1 teaspoon mayonnaise
salt and pepper to taste

THE PRICE OF WISDOM IS ABOVE RUBIES.

JOB 28:18

Happiness is found within your heart and not in any external luxuries. Wisdom is the tool which enables you to analyze everything with sweet eyes, benefit of the doubt, and joy, making every situation and moment feel more precious than rubies. With happiness in your heart and wisdom in your decisions, joy and completion will accompany you through all of the high and low points of your life. The greatest diamond to chase is that of happiness, and you can find true happiness by possessing the wisdom of knowing that everything is good, because everything is from God. We cannot take rubies to heaven with us, but surely the positive wisdom that we acquired from the bible during our lifetime will be the angel's wings that escort our souls to the higher worlds.

Egg Salad

In my house, egg salad is the one dish that I know all three of my picky kids will eat. My neighbor has a chicken coup in his yard, so I often take my kids to the coup and find fresh organic eggs that we go home to cook and eat. There are so many variations of egg salad, but this recipe is my family's favorite.

INGREDIENTS

4 eggs, hard boiled
2 tablespoons mayonnaise
¼ onions, chopped
½ teaspoon salt
pepper
½ teaspoon sweet paprika

- Mash the hard boiled eggs.

- One by one, add the remaining ingredients in the order listed.

Delicious on a cracker or sandwich, and a side dish that goes with everything!

delicious seed mix

Delicious Seed Mix

This mix is my husband's invention that has led to a 'seed mix addiction' on my part. This seed mix tastes so delicious on everything; I sprinkle it on all of my salads, mix it into rice dishes, eat it on bread with a little butter, and even top my breakfast eggs with these seeds. The mixture stays good for a long time, so sometimes we will make double or triple the recipe…it always gets eaten in the end!

INGREDIENTS

⅓ cup pumpkin seeds
¼ cup sunflower seeds
1 tablespoon white sesame seeds
1 tablespoon black sesame seeds
2 tablespoons flax seeds

- Warm up a medium size pan over a medium heat (without oil).

- Place all of the seeds in the pan over a low flame, mix constantly for 3-5 minutes, until the seeds are turning a light brown color.

- Sprinkle a little salt on the seeds and mix (optional).

- Before serving, mix a little olive oil with the seeds (optional).

Store in tupperware for up to two weeks, and sprinkle the seed mixture over salads, on sandwiches, and any of your favorite dishes.

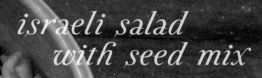

israeli salad

israeli salad
with seed mix

Israeli Salad

My husband is Israeli and I clearly remember being at his parents' house and offering to help his mother make a salad. She sent me to the fridge to get out the vegetables and when I saw there was no lettuce in the vegetable drawer I was totally confused. "How will we make a salad without lettuce," I asked her, dumbfounded. Well, apparently Israeli salads are lettuce free! The trick to an Israeli salad is to take lots of vegetables and chop them up very small, then drizzle a simple and healthy dressing on top which consists of olive oil, lemon juice, and salt/pepper. You'll never believe how delicious (and colorful!) this wonderful salad comes out.

INGREDIENTS

2 cucumbers
1 red pepper
1 scallion stalk
2 carrots
2 pickles
parsley, chopped (optional)

DRESSING

¼ cup olive oil
juice from half of a fresh lemon
salt and pepper to taste

- Finely chop all of the vegetables and place in a bowl.

- Mix together the salad dressing, and pour onto the salad immediately before serving.

PESTO

This traditional Italian dip has kind of been adopted in the Middle East. When I make Shabbat meals, we always start the meal with a 'salad course' which consists of Challah (bread), lots of dips —including pesto—, and one fresh vegetable salad. On top of using pesto for a bread dip, you can mix it with pasta to make a 'pesto pasta' dish. Yummmm, delicious!

INGREDIENTS

1 large bunch of basil, leaves only, washed and dried
3 medium cloves garlic
½ cup pine nuts
¼ cup sunflower seeds
½ cup parmesan cheese, loosely packed and freshly grated (optional)
¼ cup extra-virgin olive oil

- Put all ingredients in a food processor, and blend until it is all mixed together and smooth.

Pesto tastes delicious on bread or crackers, on pasta, salad, or rice, and as a dip for veggies.

Depart from evil, and do good; seek peace, and pursue it

Psalm 34:14

A meaningful life is a life of purpose and intention. We must do good, seek peace, actively pursue the things in life that matter. Nothing of value just happens. We must be active participants in the drama of living well. What matters to you most? What is of ultimate value? Never stop working on yourself and striving towards more conscious living. It is the examined life that leads toward fulfillment and joy.

Shredded Beet
& Carrot Salad

I love serving colorful and healthy salads before serving the main course because it makes the table look beautiful and everyone always fills up on them (which is the healthiest part of the meal!). This stunning and delicious salad is so easy to make, and will truly be the conversation piece. I often put together this salad last minute to add an extra dish to my planned meal.

Ingredients

2 beets
3 carrots
2 celery stalks
2 tablespoons olive oil
1 tablespoon lemon juice
salt and pepper to taste

- In a food processor, with shredder insert, shred beets and carrots.

- Chop the celery stalks by hand and mix together with beet and carrot mixture.

- Dress the salad immediately before serving with olive oil, lemon juice, salt, and pepper.

Spinach & Strawberry Salad

This salad always makes me think of summer, even if I'm serving it in the dead of winter. Who doesn't like strawberries in their salad? This salad is sweet and delicious, and is the perfect way to get those picky eaters to get their healthy serving of spinach.

INGREDIENTS

1 pound fresh spinach
1 pint strawberries, sliced
1 cup pecans, sugared
½ red onion, sliced

DRESSING

¾ cup sugar
⅓ cup vinegar
¼ cup poppy seeds
1 teaspoon salt
1½ tablespoons onion, grated
1 teaspoon dry mustard
1 cup olive oil

- Combine spinach, pecans, onions, and strawberries in bowl. In a blender, mix sugar, vinegar, poppy seed, salt, dry mustard, and onion. Slowly add the oil. Pour over salad.

So teach us to number our days, that we may apply our hearts unto wisdom.

Psalm 90:12

Don't feel rushed in anything you do and fill each project with your whole being. Take your time and think about every action, so that not one moment of life passes by wasted. Wisdom is acquired when we learn from each step of every experience; it is then we realize that there is no such thing as failure, disappointment or waste. Each new day is a blessing from God, and an opportunity to learn, discover, and grow. Who is one that possesses wisdom? Wisdom is possessed by those who learn and find deep lessons in the seemingly mundane hustle and bustle of day to day living.

Sweet & Salty Spinach Salad

I love salads based on spinach, and anything with cheese as an ingredient is a dish that I'll eat. This salad is so delicious that you'll never believe it is healthy too!

INGREDIENTS

4 cups fresh spinach leaves
1 tangerine, cut into small pieces
¼ cup sunflower seeds, salted
¼ cup cranberries
1 whole avocado, cubed
¼ cup crumbled feta cheese (optional)

DRESSING

1½ tablespoons balsamic vinegar
3 tablespoons extra virgin olive oil
1 teaspoon honey
1 tablespoon brown sugar
1 teaspoon dijon mustard
salt and pepper to taste

TEHINA

These days, it is easy to buy already prepared Tehina at the store, yet it cannot compete with delicious taste of homemade Tehina which takes two minutes to prepare. Tehina tastes delicious on bread (I use it instead of mayonnaise), as a dressing on salads, or as a dip for vegetables. This homemade prepared tehina will last for around a week in the fridge, but the raw tahini stays good for months. Tahina is a real Israeli food that you can easily prepare in your own kitchen.

INGREDIENTS

½ cup raw tahini
¾ cup water
juice from half of a fresh lemon
1 clove of garlic, crushed
1 teaspoon ground cumin powder
¼ teaspoon salt

- In a medium size bowl, mix together the raw tahini and water for 2 minutes. (It will be liquid, then thick, and if you continue mixing it will get to a perfect consistency.)

- Add the remaining ingredients, mix, and serve.

Tehina is delicious as a dip for bread, on salad, or as a dip for vegetables. It is a staple food in Israel that we put on everything!

ON THREE THINGS THE WORLD IS SUSTAINED: ON THE TORAH, ON THE (TEMPLE) SERVICE, AND ON DEEDS OF LOVING KINDNESS.

ETHICS OF THE FATHERS, CHAPTER 1

Ancient Jewish wisdom establishes life's priorities. Our obligation is to study and to live God's word, to serve God and to perform good deeds. The Ten Commandments are composed of five that pertain to the relationship between man and God, and five that pertain to the relationship between man and man, testament to the fact that both spiritual and physical realms are of utmost importance. To be faithful to God, it is our obligation to nurture both aspects.

"THOSE WHO HOPE IN THE LORD WILL RENEW THEIR STRENGTH. THEY WILL SOAR ON WINGS LIKE EAGLES; THEY WILL RUN AND NOT GROW WEARY, THEY WILL WALK AND NOT BE FAINT.'

ISAIAH 40:32

True strength comes from faith in the Lord. It is easy to confuse strength with other things, like power, wealth, and success. But that type of strength is fragile and ephemeral. It comes and it goes, it disappoints. Faith in God sustains us through life and survives life's challenges. Only faith in God gives strength that can heal the sick, power to conquer our fears and the stamina to pursue our dreams. It's the kind of strength that grows with age and doesn't diminish.

TOMATO MOZERELLA SALAD

This simple salad is so quick to prepare and is unbelievably delicious. I love eating it for a light lunch throughout the week. I grow my own basil in our garden outside, so my kids love picking the basil leaves from the plant and then putting them directly into the salad.

INGREDIENTS

15 cherry tomatoes, halved
10 leaves fresh basil
5 black olives, halved and pitted
½ cup mozzarella, cubed

DRESSING

1 tablespoon olive oil
½ tablespoon balsamic vinegar
salt and pepper to taste

**KNOW THEREFORE THAT THE LORD
YOUR GOD IS GOD, THE FAITHFUL GOD
WHO KEEPS COVENANT AND STEADFAST
LOVE WITH THOSE WHO LOVE HIM AND
KEEP HIS COMMANDMENTS,
TO A THOUSAND GENERATIONS**

DEUTERONOMY 7:9

God's word is eternal and he will be faithful forever to those who love him and live by His word. His presence is not always obvious. In fact there are times that He feels hidden and we feel alone. It is for us to establish God's presence in our heart and in the world. Do something for someone else, help someone out, give of yourself - see how quickly you feel His presence all around you

GRAINS
& SIDES

THE NAME OF THE LORD IS A STRONG FORTRESS; THE GODLY RUN TO HIM AND ARE SAFE.

PROVERBS 18:10

How can a name offer protection? The real question is, if we are not with God, how can anything or anyone promise us safety? The only path to real safety and security is a life of faith, charity and good deeds. When we understand that true protection is only from the Lord, and that He is always waiting for us to return to him, we call out his Name and know that he is with us.

Asian Brown Rice

This is a delicious and quick rice dish that is bursting with flavor and goes with everything.

Ingredients

1 tablespoon ginger, chopped
5 cloves garlic, chopped
oil for sautéing
1 cup brown rice
2 cups water
¼ cup canned corn
¼ cup canned peas
½ teaspoon salt
1 tablespoon toasted sesame oil

- In a medium pot, sauté chopped ginger and garlic in oil.

- Add brown rice and water.

- Once it is boiling, put in corn, peas, and salt. Cover.

- Simmer and cook rice.

- Add toasted sesame oil.

Baked Egg Rolls

Seriously…who doesn't like egg rolls?? I love egg rolls, but up until one of my friends shared this special recipe with me, it was a guilty pleasure. These egg rolls are not fried, but baked, and taste amazing!

Ingredients

 1 package Moroccan cigar filo dough
 2 cups each of shredded cabbage and carrots
 1 package sprouts of your choice
 2 tablespoons vinegar
 1 tablespoon honey
 2 tablespoons soy sauce

 • Preheat oven to 375°F.

 • Sauté veggies together with sauce (all remaining ingredients except for filo dough).

 • Put into dough and roll into egg roll.

 • Bake on 190°C/375°F until golden brown.

"FOR I KNOW THE PLANS I HAVE FOR YOU," DECLARES THE LORD, "PLANS TO PROSPER YOU AND NOT TO HARM YOU, PLANS TO GIVE YOU HOPE AND A FUTURE.

JEREMIAH 29:11

When we are going through difficult and trying times, it can feel like God has forgotten or abandoned us. Throughout our hardships, it is critical to remember that God is in control and loves us unconditionally. When you wake up in the morning and before you go to sleep, remind yourself that you are dear to God, and that He is with you during every moment of every day. Next time things do not go your way or you receive difficult news, take a moment to remember this verse and feel in your heart that God has His divine plans and everything that happens is only for the best.

BROCCOLI CASSEROLE

This broccoli casserole is sooooo delicious. I make it as a side dish often and have yet to have leftovers. You will be super surprised by the bursting flavor in this casserole and will definitely use this recipe often. Enjoy!

INGREDIENTS

½ bag frozen broccoli, thawed
1½ tablespoons olive oil
1½ tablespoons flour
3 eggs
½ cup mayonnaise
2 tablespoons onion soup mix *or* one sautéd onion
½ teaspoon salt
½ cup soy milk
1 cup corn flakes
½ cup honey

- Preheat oven to 375°F.

- Mix all ingredients (other than corn flakes and honey) until mixed together and pour into greased pan.

- Cover the top with cornflakes and drizzle with honey.

- Bake for 45 minutes on 190°C/375°F.

Bulgar Tabouli

This delicious and ethnic recipe is one of my husband's favorites. It is healthy, has tons of flavor, and can be prepared the day before you want to serve it (which gets some cooking out of the way beforehand). This makes a great light lunch and saves well in the fridge.

Ingredients

1 cup raw bulgar
1 cup lemon juice
⅔ cup olive oil
5 cloves garlic, crushed
salt and pepper to taste
6-8 scallions, chopped
2 handfuls of parsley
⅓ cup mint, chopped
5 tomatoes, with seeds removed

- Mix together bulgar, lemon juice, olive oil, garlic, salt, and pepper.

- Add scallions, parsley, mint, tomatoes.

- Let sit in fridge until the bulgur gets soft and serve!

carrot kugel bread

CARROT KUGEL BREAD

I serve this carrot bread with the meal as a side dish, yet it truly tastes like desert. It is easy to prepare and delicious to eat…my type of food!

INGREDIENTS

2 cups flour
1½ cup sugar
2 teaspoons baking powder
1 teaspoon baking soda
1 teaspoon cinnamon
3 carrots, shredded
⅔ cup orange juice
3 tablespoons lemon juice
4 eggs
1 teaspoons salt

- Preheat oven to 325°F.

- Mix all ingredients together and pour in greased loaf pan.

- Bake at 350°F for 50-60 minutes (until a toothpick comes out clean when you stick it in the middle).

Coconut Milk Rice

This is my favorite rice dish in the world. The creamy texture and mixture of tastes leaves it the most delicious rice dish I have ever tasted. With the beautiful colors and mouthwatering smells, everyone in the house will be counting down the minutes until it is done.

INGREDIENTS

2 cups basmati rice
2 cups coconut cream or canned coconut liquid
2 cups water
¼ cup fresh dill, chopped
salt and pepper
½ teaspoon garlic powder
1 tablespoon tumeric powder
2 cinnamon sticks

- Put all ingredients together in a pot, boil uncovered, then cover and simmer until there is no water left and rice is soft (around 10 minutes).

- After the rice is cooked, top with a little bit of soy sauce and enjoy!

BE STRONG AND COURAGEOUS. DO NOT BE AFRAID OR TERRIFIED BECAUSE OF THEM, FOR THE LORD YOUR GOD GOES WITH YOU; HE WILL NEVER LEAVE YOU NOR FORSAKE YOU."

DEUTERONOMY 31:6

There are many different personal and universal events that can cause a person anxiety or fear. Everywhere we turn we are bombarded with news of tragedies, wars, and suffering, and it is difficult to maintain the feeling of courage and strength. The only way to eliminate fear from your heart is to know that God is with you, and is stronger than your enemies. When you turn to God, He answers, and when you allow Him into your life, He is present. God is reliable, constant, and full of love for you. So always remember to stay strong and courageous because you have nothing to fear!

THY WORD IS A LAMP TO MY FEET, AND A LIGHT TO MY PATH.

PSALMS 119:105

Through our speech we have the ability to change someone's entire reality. When you see someone is sad, tell them nice things. Say 'Hello' next time you throw a dollar into a beggar's cup. Teach your children a trade that they enjoy. Explain your intentions to a person you annoy. Speak out loud to yourself to overcome your problems, confusion and worry. Light your own path, along with others, through the power of speech.

CREAMY & CHEESY POTATOES

Cheesy potatoes is definitely on my list of 'top 5 favorite foods' and I've been testing out different recipes to make this mouthwateringly delicious dish perfect. This is a recipe that I put together after trying lots of different variations, and it tastes divine. Get your fingers ready for licking!

INGREDIENTS

8 potatoes
1 can coconut milk or liquid
salt and pepper to taste
paprika to taste
2 cups cheddar cheese, shredded, for topping

- Preheat oven to 450°F.

- Cut potatoes in small, thin pieces and pour coconut milk over them. Top with salt, pepper, and paprika.

- Bake covered at 450°F for around 35 minutes or until the potatoes are soft.

- Take the potatoes out of oven and sprinkle shredded cheddar cheese on top, bake uncovered for another 10 minutes.

Parsley & Garlic Green Beans

These green beans are so delicious and also fun to eat! When I make this recipe, the entire house smells so good that everyone is waiting by the stove for them to be ready. They truly do taste as good as they smell!

INGREDIENTS

2 pounds fresh green beans *or* one frozen package
1 cup water
1 head garlic, chopped
1 tablespoon oil
½ teaspoon salt
⅛ teaspoon pepper
1 cup fresh parsley, chopped

- Wash green beans; trim ends and remove any strings.

- Bring water to a boil in large saucepan. Add beans.

- Cover, reduce heat to medium and cook 10 minutes, stirring occasionally.

- Drain and set aside.

- While youre waiting for the beans to cook, warm up the oil in large skillet.

- Once oil is warm, add garlic and cook until it is soft (4 minutes); add the green beans. Stir in parsley, salt, and pepper. Cook over medium heat 3 minutes or until thoroughly heated, stirring occasionally.

Pesto Basmatti

This basmati rice is so simple, yet delicious. I like using fresh homemade pesto in this dish, but if you don't have time to prepare the fresh pesto, you can use store bought.

INGREDIENTS

1 cup basmati rice, cooked
¼ cup pesto
½ cup parmesan cheese, shredded

- Mix all ingredients together

yellow rice

Yellow Rice

I often have lots of big families with kids over for Shabbat meals, and am very conscious of needing to make a simple dish for those picky eaters. This plain rice dish is simple enough that the picky kids like it, yet exciting enough that the adults will take some too. It goes great with everything, and will add some color to your table.

INGREDIENTS

1 tablespoon tumeric
¼ teaspoon salt
2 cups basmati rice
4 cups water

- Combine tumeric, salt, (uncooked) rice, and water.

- Bring to a boil, cover, and simmer until water is absorbed (around 10 minutes).

Potato (Kugel) Casserole

Potato kugel is a traditional side dish for Shabbat lunch meals, and boy is it delicious! This kugel (casserole) is best served with meat meals and tastes best straight out of the oven.

Ingredients

6 large potatoes
2 large onions
4 eggs
¼ cup oil
3 teaspoons salt
¼ teaspoon pepper
2 tablespoons oil

- Preheat oven to 400°F.

- Grate potatoes with onions, drain liquid

- Add eggs and stir in oil (¼ cup); mix together.

- Add salt and pepper; mix together.

- In medium sized pan, add oil (2 tablespoons) and heat in oven at 400°F for one minute.

- Take out hot pan and pour in the potato mixture. Bake uncovered at 400°F for 1 hour, until the top is slightly crispy and golden brown.

For my brethren and companions' sake, I will now ask, Peace be with thee.

Psalms 122:8

Our central focus is on our own lives, problems and thoughts, yet it is crucial to open up and think about others. It can sometimes be a challenge to truly feel happiness for someone else's success and to help them reach their goals, yet it brings completion to the heart. We are all connected in good times and bad and have the power to change someone's hardships into blessings through nice words, guidance and intention. Go out and change the world through the power of words! Bring peace to the universe!

I PUT ON RIGHTEOUSNESS,
AND IT CLOTHED ME

JOB 29:14-15

Our values are like our clothes – they cover us, they protect us, and they define us to the world. What garments do you want the world to see? Choose your values no less carefully than you choose the clothing you wear each day. Stay focused and alert to ensure that your actions clothe you in beauty and righteousness.

DAIRY & VEGAN MAIN COURSES

Chapatti Wraps

Chapatti wraps are traditionally served in Israel in place of bread. They take just a few minutes to prepare and taste delicious when stuffed with nearly anything and used as a wrap. I like cutting up lots of fresh vegetables and preparing healthy homemade dips, setting everything up in bowls on the table, and then letting my children fill their own chapatti. It's fun and delicious!

INGREDIENTS

3 cups flour
1 teaspoon salt
2-3 teaspoons oil
1 cup warm water

- Mix all ingredients together and then knead on floured surface.

- Roll into round-shaped, flat wraps.

- Warm a medium pan over a medium heat, then place the flat wraps in the pan to cook (without oil).

- Cook over medium flame for 2-3 minutes on each side.

THOU SHALT SHINE FORTH, THOU SHALT BE AS THE MORNING.

JOB 11:15-17

It is the simple miracles that we must learn to appreciate. The sun rises each morning and wards off the darkness, bringing newness and life onto the earth. Every morning we can rise like the sun and shine our unique light upon the world. Give your family, friends and people you pass in the street life by showing a smile, speaking kindly, and sharing a helpful word. Each day remember that you can be the light onto the world through by filling every mundane act with intention and joy.

BEHOLD, HOW GOOD AND HOW PLEASANT IT IS FOR BRETHREN TO DWELL TOGETHER IN UNITY!

PSALMS 133:1

Genuine respect for others is possible and attainable. Try to open up your heart to the world and all of the different colors, customs, traditions, needs and aspirations surrounding us. We must not try and change one another, but rather understand, respect and learn from everyone. Once we realize that each person on this earth is a spark of the infinite, we can appreciate our differences. Try to find a positive point in each person you don't get along with and let that point be your focus. That point is their strength that you can surely learn from.

Cheese Quiche

In my house, quiches are always a hit. With so many different cheeses and flavors, there are never any leftovers of this cheese quiche when I make it for dinner. This is a great recipe to make with little kids that love to help in the kitchen; my kids love sprinkling the cheese inside the quiche and mixing all of the ingredients together, as we sing and pray.

INGREDIENTS

2 cups cottage cheese
1 cup yogurt, plain and unsweetened
5 beat eggs
¼ cup feta cheese, crumbled
¼ cup parmesan
¼ cup cheddar
1 pie crust
¼ teaspoon salt
pepper
½ cup american cheese, grated

- Preheat oven to 400°F.

- Add all ingredients, except american cheese, together in a bowl and mix well.

- Pour the mixture in a pie crust.

- Top with ½ cup grated american cheese.

- Bake on 400°F for 25 minutes, or until the top is golden brown and the eggs are cooked.

CREAMY LASAGNA

From the time my eldest daughter could talk, she would ask me to make my special lasagna for dinner nearly every night. She won't eat lasagna in restaurants and only wants my special homemade lasagna. This recipe produces the creamiest, tastiest, most delicious lasagna which everyone will be raving about for weeks. Each time I make this lasagna I think of my daughter who loves it so much, and I integrate good thoughts and prayers into my cooking for her to ingest into her body.

INGREDIENTS

1 cup cottage cheese
1 cup yogurt, plain and unsweetened
1½ cups sweet creamer
1 jar of pasta sauce
½ teaspoon salt
1 package of lasagna noodles (no need for pre-cook)
4 cups of cheese (of your choice), shredded, separated

- Preheat oven to 400°F.

- In a bowl, mix together all ingredients except for the noodles and shredded cheese.

- In a medium size pan, place a layer of sauce, noodles, sauce, ¾ cup shredded cheese (of your choice, or a mixture). Repeat. Top off the lasagna with 1 cup shredded cheese.

- Bake covered on 400°F for 40 minutes, then cook uncovered for 15 minutes.

CREAMY PEANUT BUTTER NOODLES

When I went to college in New York, there was an Asian local restaurant that made the most delicious peanut butter noodles. For years, I tried to recreate that mouth-watering flavor in my own kitchen, and finally I found the trick. This is a great side dish for any meal and is easy to make. Everyone will be licking their lips, and coming back for more!

INGREDIENTS

1 package of spaghetti or rice soba noodles
½ cup peanut butter
3 tablespoons soy sauce
½ teaspoon lemon
½ cup veggie broth
1½ tablespoons of brown sugar
¼ teaspoon salt
1 scallion, chopped
2 tablespoons sesame seeds

- Cook rice soba noodles or traditional spaghetti according to package instructions, set aside.

- In a saucepan add together all of the ingredients except for the spaghetti, scallions, and sesame seeds.

- Turn flame on low and stir constantly for 2 minutes (until all ingredients are mixed together).

- Mix noodles and sauce together. Top with scallions and sesame seeds. Serve hot or cold.

Creamy Vegetable-Coconut Milk Pasta

I discovered this recipe one evening when I walked in from work late at night, I had three cranky kids begging me to make pasta, and I had no cheese or milk in the house. Deciding to become creative, I pulled out a can of coconut milk, chopped up all of the vegetables in my fridge, and invented a delicious recipe that my family begs me to make often. This unique pasta sauce recipe is one of the only 'guilt free' cream recipes you will find – and it tastes superb!

INGREDIENTS

  4 tablespoons olive oil
  ½ cup mushrooms, chopped
  1 onion, sliced
  ½ cup broccoli, chopped
  6 cherry tomatoes, halved
  2 cups coconut liquid, canned
  salt and pepper to taste
  ¼ teaspoon garlic powder
  1 package spaghetti

- Cook spaghetti according to instructions and put aside.

- In a big saucepan, heat olive oil.

- Add the vegetables and sauté for 10 minutes mixing constantly.

- Add coconut milk and spices to the vegetables and simmer for 10 minutes.

- Pour the sauce over the spaghetti and enjoy!

Can also be served over rice or Quinoa.

HER WAYS ARE WAYS OF PLEASANTNESS, AND ALL HER PATHS ARE PEACE.

PROVERBS 3:17

Peace is a state of mind based on energies that we tap into. When we perceive something as beautiful, that is the clothing it wears and the identity it becomes. We create our own reality and through talking kindly, performing positive acts, helping others and staying away from judgment we can create a reality of peace that follows us throughout our life. This way, if we nurture peace in our hearts and act with those intentions, we are mirroring God, and will live a peaceful, meaningful life.

Cupcake Pizza Calzone

When I bite into these delicious and savory pizza calzone cups, I'm reminded why nearly everyone in the world loves pizza…including my three Israeli children that beg me for pizza nearly every day. Here in the Holy Land it is not easy to find a good pizza restaurant, so I have resorted to making it myself. This is an easy and fun recipe to make, which tastes delicious! You can add any vegetables in the pizza cups and make it as cheesy as you like. I like the spicy flavor, so I often cut up a piece of fresh, hot chili pepper and throw it inside the calzone cup. You won't see anyone turning these away!

INGREDIENTS

1 package of filo dough cups
prepared pasta sauce in a jar
1 cup feta cheese
2 cups mozzarella cheese, shredded
fresh mushrooms, sliced or diced
salt and pepper to taste

- Preheat oven to 275°F.

- In a muffin pan line each place with filo dough.

- Place one spoonful of pasta sauce inside the filo dough, along with a small piece of feta cheese, shredded mozzarella, and a pinch of mushrooms.

- Top with half a spoon of pasta sauce, salt and pepper to taste.

- Bake on 275°F until filo dough is brown and crispy and cheese is melted (around 15 minutes).

- Let cool for 5 minutes, enjoy!

Sesame Tofu Slices

I enjoy cooking with tofu because it takes on whatever flavor and texture you want it to. I love crispy tofu with a salty flavor, and sesame seeds on top make it simply delicious! My family eats these tofu squares straight out of the pan and sometimes we throw them on top of a fresh salad which makes the salad unique, hearty, and delicious.

INGREDIENTS

14 ounces extra firm tofu
¼ cup flour, for dusting
canola oil, for frying
1 cup sesame seed, lightly toasted
1 bunch scallion, trimmed and cut into 1-inch pieces

SAUCE

⅓ cup honey
3 tablespoons tamari soy sauce
1 teaspoon ginger powder
2 tablespoons sesame oil

2 tablespoons rice vinegar
2 cloves garlic, finely minced
1 teaspoon red chili pepper flakes

- Wrap tofu with paper towels and drain liquid

- Cut the tofu into 2 inch by 2 inch, thin squares

- Stir sauce ingredients together

- Dust tofu very lightly with flour, then dip into the sauce

- Heat 1 inch of oil in deep frying pan.

- Fry tofu in oil until golden brown; turn over and make sure both sides are browned.

- Place fried tofu in a large bowl and toss with 1 cup sauce, sprinkle liberally with sesame seeds and scallions and serve hot.

shakshuka

SHAKSHUKA

Shakshuka is a traditional breakfast in Israel that I used to treat myself to at restaurants once a month when my husband and I had our monthly date morning at the local café. After craving this delicious and unique dish during my pregnancy, I decided to play around and try to make it myself. It didn't take too many tries until I realized that this unique dish is easy, healthy, tasty, and hard to get wrong. Everyone in my family gobbles this homemade shakshuka up for whatever meal I make it for, and always asks for more!

INGREDIENTS

1 tablespoon canola oil
1 onion, chopped
1 zucchini, chopped
2 cloves garlic, chopped
2 tomatoes, diced
10 ounce jar of pasta sauce
5 eggs

- In a large pan, over a medium heat, heat the oil.

- Add the onion, zucchini, and garlic; sauté until they are soft and onions are a little browned.

- Add tomatoes and sauté for another 3 minutes, mixing.

- Add pasta sauce to the vegetable mixture over a low flame and mix. Wait for it to boil.

- While it is boiling, crack eggs on top of the mixture. Let it boil for 10 minutes until the white part of the egg is cooked. Serve with bread.

Tip: After the eggs are cracked on top of the tomato mixture, use a spatula to make little holes in the tomato mixture to let the white part of the eggs seep through and get cooked.

Optional: sprinkle feta cheese on top

Tasty & Delicious Lentils

Before making this recipe, it was simply a dream of mine that my children would beg me for healthy food for dinner. This lentil recipe is so tasty and delicious that majadra (lentils and rice) is my children's second favorite food, coming in close after lasagna. I love eating this healthy and tasty dish for lunch or dinner and leftovers heat up perfectly.

INGREDIENTS

1 tablespoon canola oil
1 onion, sliced
2 carrots, chopped
4 cloves garlic, chopped
2 celery stalks, chopped
½ cup ketchup
1 teaspoon curry
1 tablespoon soy sauce
1 tablespoon brown sugar
1 cup lentils
3 cups water

- In a medium size pot, heat canola oil.

- In the warm oil, sauté the onion, carrots, garlic, and celery; mix for two minutes over medium heat.

- Add ketchup, curry, soy sauce, sugar, and salt; mix together with vegetables for 2 minutes over medium heat.

- Add lentils and water, mix.

- Boil, then set on low flame for around an hour until lentils are soft. Add more water as needed.

- Serve with brown or white rice and top with feta cheese (optional).

tasty &
delicious lentils

veggie noodle stir fry

Veggie Noodle Stir Fry

I love simple and healthy meals that are easy to prepare and bursting with flavor. This dish completely meets those standards and is definitely one of my favorite dinner dishes.

Ingredients

4 tablespoons olive oil
2 cups purple cabbage, chopped
2 scallions, chopped
5 cloves garlic, chopped
1 carrot, chopped
1 cup mung bean sprouts
½ teaspoon ginger powder
2 tablespoons soy sauce
1 tablespoon sugar
1 package spaghetti noodles, broken in half before cooking

- Cook spaghetti noodles according to package instructions until they are almost done (still a little hard). Put aside.

- In a wok or big sauce pan, heat olive oil.

- Add the chopped garlic to the pan and sauté until it is golden brown.

- Add the cooked noodles and veggies, then simmer on medium heat for 10 minutes, stirring often.

Spinach Cheese Quiche

I love making quiches for dinner, and I even make a few extras during my free time to place in the freezer for a busy day, when I have no time to cook a warm meal for my family. This quiche recipe always comes out perfect and delicious, and is a great way to sneak in the important spinach vitamins. After seeing how easy this recipe is and how delicious it comes out, you'll never order quiche at a restaurant again!

INGREDIENTS

2 cups cottage cheese
1 cup yogurt, plain
5 eggs, beat together
1 onion, sliced
3 tablespoons pine nuts
½ cup frozen spinach, thawed and drained
¼ cup feta cheese, crumbled
¼ teaspoon salt
pepper
1 pie crust
1 cup mozzarella cheese, grated

- Preheat oven to 400°F.

- Add all ingredients except mozzarella cheese together in a bowl and mix well.

- Pour the mixture in a pie crust

- Top with grated mozzarella cheese.

- Bake on 400°F for 25 minutes, or until the top is golden brown and the eggs are cooked.

I had rather be a doorkeeper in the house of my God

Psalms 84:10

Value today is judged in terms of financial worth, and a successful person is defined as one who has achieved great wealth. Redefine the meaning of success for yourself in terms of the joy something brings you, the peace you feel in your heart and the happiness that accommodates your every step. Choose a profession based on your passions and joys and hang around people that accentuate your good points, make you laugh and feel good. Don't be bothered by stature and strive to live in the vision of your truth.

Better is a dinner of herbs where love is, than a stalled ox and hatred therewith.

Proverbs 15:17

The outcome of our toil is based on the intentions that we fill it with. If you are content within yourself and surroundings, joy and tranquility will follow you through all the journeys of your life. When you toil with positive thinking, love, and an open heart, there is no such thing as failure. Failure, anger and hatred are all relative and based on your state of mind. Put loving intentions into everything you do, stay positive and when something breaks pick up the pieces. Failure will be a thing of the past. Simplicity and love are two Godly values that can guide our way to true accomplishment and joy.

CHICKEN

bursting with flavor
traditional chicken & potatoes

BURSTING WITH FLAVOR
TRADITIONAL
CHICKEN & POTATOES

Chicken and potatoes is a traditional Shabbat main course for Jewish families around the world. This simple – yet delicious – dish began to become a staple Shabbat food in Eastern Europe, where potatoes are easy to grow. To this day, Jews around the world continue to make this special dish. Watching my children devour the chicken and potatoes fills my heart with joy, and gives them the special feeling of home, warmth, and connecting to our past. This is a delicious and flavorful dish that takes little time to prepare. You can serve the chicken and potatoes together or in separate serving pieces.

INGREDIENTS

1 whole chicken, cut into 8 pieces
4 white potatoes, cubed
1 onion, sliced
1½ tablespoons paprika
1½ tablespoons garlic powder
½ teaspoon salt
pinch of pepper
1 cup olive oil

- Preheat oven to 425°F.

- Place the chicken and all ingredients in a cooking bag and mix it together.

- Place the closed chicken bag in big baking dish.

- Bake at 425°F for 1 hour. Turn the cooking bag over after 30 minutes.

Chicken Teryaki

The delicious mix of soy sauce and honey is one of my favorite flavors in the world. When I'm in a rush for time yet want to make a special and delicious main course that everyone loves – including professional collogues, my husband, and my three picky kids – this is the recipe I use. A mixture of salty and sweet flavors leaves everyone licking their fingers, and no one will believe that you made this sauce from scratch!

Ingredients

5 pieces of boned and halved chicken breast
¼ cup canola oil
½ cup soy sauce
½ cup honey
4 cloves garlic, crushed
2 teaspoons lemon juice
1 tablespoon sesame seeds

- Preheat oven to 375°F.

- In a medium cooking dish, lay out the pieces of chicken.

- Mix together all ingredients except for the sesame seeds and pour over the chicken.

- Cook in oven uncovered for 10 minutes.

- Turn over the chicken pieces and spinkle the sesame seeds on top, then continue cooking for another 15 minutes.

chicken teryaki

Delicious Creamy Chicken Stew

I keep a strictly kosher home, which means that I never cook with meat and milk together. In this creamy chicken dish, I substitute coconut milk for cream, and the taste is simply divine! All of these marvelous flavors combined will make you go for seconds and thirds. This stew is a fun food that my kids love to eat over rice. On late work nights, this is my 'go to' dish; easy to prepare, healthy, and delicious. You simply can't go wrong!

INGREDIENTS

1½ tablespoons oil
4 cloves garlic, chopped
1 onion, diced
5 boned chicken breasts, cut into 1-inch pieces
1 can diced tomatoes, undrained
1 can chickpeas, drained
1 can coconut cream/liquid
1 teaspoon salt
1 teaspoon curry
1 teaspoon soy sauce

- In a large saucepan, heat oil.

- Sauté garlic and onion, until onion is clear.

- Add chicken and sauté for another 2-3 minutes until the outside of the chicken is white.

- Add tomatoes, chickpeas, coconut cream, salt, curry, and soy sauce; mix.

- Cover and simmer for 20 minutes, mixing every five minutes.

- Serve hot over white basmati rice.

Chicken Stir Fry with Teryaki Sauce

This delicious stir fry with fresh ginger and garlic is bursting with flavor. The perfect alternative to Chinese take-out, this dish is quick to prepare, healthy, and delicious. It also warms up very well, so save those leftovers!

Ingredients

2 tablespoons canola oil
4 cloves garlic, chopped
1 tablespoon ginger, freshly chopped
1 onion, sliced
3 skinless, boneless chicken breast halves, thinly sliced
half a bag of frozen broccoli, thawed
4 tablespoons soy sauce
2 teaspoons brown sugar
salt and pepper

- In a large saucepan or wok, warm canola oil.

- Add garlic, ginger, and onion; sauté on medium flame while stirring until onion is soft (around 5 minutes).

- Add 3 skinless, boneless chicken breast halves, thinly sliced and sauté for 3-5 minutes, until the outside of the chicken looks white and cooked.

- Add broccoli and pour on soy sauce, brown sugar, and salt to taste; mix.

- Leave stir fry over flame for another 10-15 minutes, or until the chicken is cooked through.

- Can be served alone as a chicken dish or over rice.

Pleasant words are as a honeycomb, sweet to the soul, and health to the bones.

Proverbs 16:24

When you are happy or love someone, express it. Use your words to create positivity in the world and set an example of how important communication and expression is. Often times we boldly express our concern, anger or disappointment during difficult times, yet forget to express our joy, thanksgiving, and excitement during positive moments. Putting feelings into words makes them real, and gives everyone around you the gift of sharing in your deepest emotions. Your insides will glow with positivity and joy after telling a lover what they mean to you, a parent how much you care, a child how proud you are of them, or a stranger how beautiful their smile is. Give it a try!

HONEY BAKED CHICKEN

This is my mother's recipe which my sisters and I used to beg her to make every week for Shabbat. This honey chicken is a sweet variation of the traditional Israeli 'shnitzel' or fried chicken, yet it is battered and baked instead of fried. Whenever my mother would make this dish, we would all go back to the baking dish with our spoon and take extra sweet cornflake sauce; we just couldn't get enough of it! Now, my children do the same thing when I make this sweet, hearty, delicious chicken.

INGREDIENTS

6 bone-in pieces of chicken, thighs, legs, or breast
2 cups canola oil
2 cups of lightly seasoned corn flake crumbs
1 cup honey

- Preheat oven to 350°F.

- Dip chicken pieces into a bowl of oil, and then coat with lightly seasoned corn flake crumbs.

- Bake uncovered at 350°F for 30 minutes.

- Drizzle honey over the chicken then continue baking until done (another 15-20 minutes depending on size).

Sweet, moist, and delicious!

HONEY MUSTARD CHICKEN

This is my husband's favorite chicken dish and I love making it because it takes nearly no time to prepare and I always have the ingredients in the fridge. There are rarely any leftovers, yet when there are, I take the chicken off the bone and throw it in a salad for a chicken salad the next day. This chicken is truly finger licking delicious!

INGREDIENTS

3 chicken breast halves
3 chicken drumsticks
¼ cup mustard
½ cup mayonnaise
juice from one lemon
¼ cup honey
3 cloves garlic, crushed
¼ cup olive oil
salt to taste
3 tablespoons oil

- Preheat oven to 375°F.

- Mix all ingredients together and pour onto chicken.

- Bake uncovered for 30 minutes at 375°F, baste chicken in sauce after 15 minutes.

Juicy Whole Chicken

When I was growing up in Chicago my mother used to make this recipe with turkey and she was famous for making the best turkey in our neighborhood. Here in Israel it is nearly impossible to find turkey, so I tried her recipe with chicken and it is equally delicious. This recipe produces the softest, juiciest, most delicious chicken I have ever tasted and leftovers warm up beautifully.

Ingredients

1 cup chicken broth
1-4 pound whole chicken, rinsed and patted dry
½ cup margarine, cut into 1 tablespoon-sized pieces
2 navel oranges, halved

salt and pepper to taste
2 cloves garlic, minced
½ cup margarine, melted
paprika

- Preheat oven to 350°F. Pour a little chicken broth into a small roasting pan, and set aside.

- Loosen the skin from the breasts and thighs of the chicken. Stuff the margarine pieces evenly underneath the skin of the chicken, and place into the roasting pan.

- Squeeze the orange halves over the chicken. Rub in the minced garlic then sprinkle the chicken with salt and pepper to taste and lots of paprika. Drizzle the melted margarine all over the chicken

- Cover the dish in a loose dome with aluminum foil, and bake in the preheated oven for 20 minutes.

- Uncover and baste the chicken with the pan juices. Continue cooking until the chicken is no longer pink, or until a meat thermometer inserted into the thickest part of the thigh reads 165°F/74°C, 1 to 2 hours. Baste the chicken every 10 minutes after you uncover it.

- Once cooked, allow the chicken to rest out of the oven for 10 minutes before slicing.

Momma's Oriental Chicken Noodle Salad

Growing up in Chicago, my mother always had delicious hot food on the table and in the oven. Yet after tasting this cold chicken noodle salad, my sisters and I would beg her to just make this meal for dinner…nearly every night! To this day, when I go back to my mom's house, this is the special dish that I ask her to make. There is so much flavor, nutrients, and love in this recipe that it is a sure hit for your family and any guests.

INGREDIENTS

1 can chicken broth
2 cups water
1-3 pound white meat boneless chicken, broiled, grilled or baked and cut up

DRESSING

¼ cup oriental sesame oil
¼ cup vegetable oil
2 tablespoons soy sauce
2 tablespoons brown sugar
½ teaspoons salt
½ teaspoons pepper

SALAD

1 red yellow pepper, cut into fine strips
1 yellow pepper, cut into fine strips
1½ cups cabbage, diced
⅓ cup carrot, diced
1 cup celery, diced
12 snow pea pods
½ pound linguine, cooked

GARNISH

½ cup green onions
1 tablespoon sesame seeds, roasted

- Mix the salad together, top with chicken (hot or cold), pour over it the dressing, and garnish.

THERE IS NOTHING BETTER FOR A MAN, THAN THAT HE SHOULD EAT AND DRINK, AND THAT HE SHOULD MAKE HIS SOUL ENJOY GOOD IN HIS LABOR.

ECCLESIASTES 2:24

We must put pleasure and intention back into the simple things in life. Take a moment to think about the fruit, vegetables, water, food that we ingest and where they originally came from; the earth. With everything being so complex in this technological era, and mankind yearning for the next revolutionary gadget, don't disconnect from the royalty of the earth and the riches she gives us. Find happiness and completion in small simple, seemingly mundane, acts like eating and drinking.

middle eastern
sweet fruit chicken

MIDDLE EASTERN SWEET FRUIT CHICKEN

In the yard of my house we have a beautiful orange tree, walnut tree, and mango tree that we care for and love. During harvest season, I put these fresh fruits and nuts into nearly every dish and thank God for the bounty that He creates. I love eating fresh food that was grown locally with love; it carries with it a very special energy!

INGREDIENTS

3 bone-in chicken breast halves and 3 chicken drumsticks
½ cup olive oil
1 cup date honey
¼ cup dried cranberries
8 dates, halved and pitted
½ cup walnuts
¼ cup almonds, slivered
1 teaspoon garlic powder
2 tablespoons brown sugar
¼ teaspoon cinnamon
1 cup of fresh orange juice *or* juice from 1 fresh orange.

- Pre-heat oven to 400°F.

- Place the chicken in a medium size baking dish and pour the orange juice over it.

- Cover the raw chicken with olive oil and date honey. (You can buy date honey at a specialty Middle Eastern food store or make it yourself. Recipe is on next page.)

- Sprinkle on top of the chicken and in between pieces: dried cranberries, fresh halved dates, walnuts, and slivered almonds.

- Sprinkle over the chicken mixture salt, pepper, garlic powder, brown sugar, and cinnamon.

- Bake covered at 400°F for 45 minutes to an hour, baste the chicken with sauce, then cook uncovered for 10 minutes.

Date Honey Recipe
Makes one cup of Date Honey

8 dates, make sure you buy the fat, sticky Medjool dates
juice of ½ a lemon, remove the seeds
½ cup water
½ cup sugar

- Remove the pit from the dates and quarter them.

- Mash the dates with a fork into a paste-like consistency.

- Add the date mash to a small sauce pan.

- Add the lemon juice water and heat over a low flame, stirring frequently with a wooden spoon (about 3 minutes).

- After the water is absorbed, add the sugar. The mash should take on a slightly more liquid quality, like butter.

- Continue stirring, adding small amounts of additional water and sugar necessary until you reach a thick goo consistency.

Sweet & Savory Apricot Mustard Chicken

In this chicken dish, the mixture of apricot jelly, brown sugar, and mustard makes your taste buds explode with joy. This is one of my favorite chicken dishes for Shabbat because it is easy to prepare and everyone loves it!

INGREDIENTS

6-8 pieces of boned chicken (legs, thighs, and/or breast)
½ cup canola oil
¼ cup soy sauce
1½ tablespoons mustard
4 tablespoons apricot jelly
1 teaspoon lemon juice
2 tablespoons brown sugar

- Preheat oven to 375°F.

- Mix together all of the ingredients and pour over chicken, in a medium baking dish.

- Cook for 45 minutes uncovered, and baste chicken in the sauce halfway through.

sweet & creamy
  peanut butter chicken

Sweet & Creamy Peanut Butter Chicken

My children eat peanut butter with everything. Every day they take peanut butter sandwiches to school, they dip vegetables in peanut butter for snack time, and they even put peanut butter in cookies and cakes that I bake. After trying to create a delicious chicken recipe that integrates my children's love for peanut butter, my addiction to soy sauce, and satisfies my husband's sweet tooth, I finally succeeded. Try this special recipe out – you won't regret it!

INGREDIENTS

8 pieces of boned chicken (legs and/or thighs/breast)
½ cup olive oil
½ cup peanut butter
1½ tablespoons soy sauce
1 teaspoon lemon juice
1 teaspoon garlic powder *or* crushed garlic
1 teaspoon salt
3 tablespoons brown sugar
1 tablespoon sesame seeds

- Preheat oven to 375°F.

- Mix together all sauce ingredients (everything except sesame seeds) and pour sauce over chicken in a medium baking dish.

- Top with sesame seeds.

- Bake at 375°F uncovered for 25-30 minutes, baste chicken in sauce after 15 minutes and continue cooking.

Sweet Vegetable Chicken

This delicious chicken has a sauce that always leaves my family licking their fingers. The chicken comes out juicy and perfect and the extra vegetable sauce tastes great on rice or to be used as a dip with bread. One of the highlights of my week is going vegetable shopping at the local farmers market, then I come home and try to integrate these healthy and fresh vegetables into any dish I can. This vegetable chicken dish is truly one of my favorites. With a taste so delicious, none of this dish will go to waste!

INGREDIENTS

6-8 pieces of boned chicken breast
2 heads of garlic, cloved
2 tomatoes, diced
3 celery stalks, chopped
1 zucchini, chopped
1 onion, sliced
1 sweet potato, thinly sliced
4 tablespoons balsamic vinegar
½ cup brown sugar
1 tablespoon mustard
¼ cup olive oil

- Preheat oven to 375°F.

- In a large baking dish, lay out the chicken with one piece next to the other.

- Place all of the vegetables and garlic on top of and around the chicken.

- Mix together the balsamic vinegar, brown sugar, mustard, and olive oil and pour over the chicken and vegetables.

- Bake uncovered at 375°F for 20-25 minutes. Baste the chicken in the sauce after 15 minutes.

- Serve alone or with basmati rice.

Through singing Your songs, my soul will be satisfied as with the richest of foods;

Psalm 63:5

Whenever I feel an overwhelming emotion boiling inside of me, I make up a song and sing it out loud. Joy, love, anger, hate, aggravation, discontent are all emotions of the heart that yearn to be understood. Without thinking about the words or tune, begin singing what's on your heart. It is a freeing feeling which takes the heaviness off of your soul. The key to building a foundation of happiness and joy is singing during your darkest moments. Next time you feel stressed, try humming a tune. Whenever I cook, whether I feel happy or rushed, I always sing.

"GRAY HAIR IS A CROWN OF SPLENDOR; IT IS ATTAINED BY A RIGHTEOUS LIFE."

PROVERBS 16:31

What values will you hold dear in your old age? What actions can you perform now, in order to be able to look back at your life when you are old and feel proud of what you have accomplished? Material possessions are important to acquire and work for, yet it is not what will make your legacy. Kindness, charity, happiness and family values are some of the wondrous deeds that will leave an influence and impression on the world, your family and friends. The details that bog us down in our daily life are not the important points to focus on or the problems that we will remember in our old age. Righteousness is attained, not acquired.

FISH

REMEMBER THE DAYS OF OLD, CONSIDER THE YEARS OF MANY GENERATIONS.

DEUT. 32:7

Tradition connects us to something deeper than ourselves. It is the values that our ancestors held dear and yearned to pass down to us and our children. The gem of tradition should be treasured and treated as the guiding force in our life. Think about the past generations that were threatened, persecuted and killed while protecting their traditions and faith, and then recognize how lucky we are to have the ability to practice our faith and traditions in freedom. Values are the lessons that you yearn to pass on to your children and can only be conveyed through actions. Recognize the freedoms, comforts and security that you feel and give thanks to previous generations for laying that foundation. Remember the days of old, and carry their lessons with you always.

Bursting with Flavor Tuna Patties

These tuna patties have been one of my favorite meals for years and my entire family eats them all up whenever I make them for dinner. They are so flavorful and healthy, yet easy and quick to make. My family likes dipping them in ketchup, or making a tuna patty sandwich with bread and veggies.

Ingredients

2 cans tuna
1 egg
½ cup cornflake crumbs
½ onion, chopped
1 clove garlic, minced
1 tablespoon soy sauce
½ tablespoon sugar
2 tablespoons ketchup
1 teaspoon sesame oil
½ teaspoon black pepper
¾ cup flour
3 cups oil, for frying

- Heat oil in a deep frying pan over a medium heat.

- Mix all ingredients in a bowl.

- Form into small, round patties.

- Fry on both sides until golden brown.

Cheddar Tilapia

Here in Israel, it is easy to find fresh cheeses. My neighbors all have goats and chickens and whenever we need fresh cheese or eggs we just walk over to their home and buy directly from them. Cheddar cheese is one of my favorite flavors, and this tilapia recipe is mouth watering perfect!

INGREDIENTS

8 tilapia fillets
1 cup cheddar, shredded
¼ cup yogurt, plain and unsweetened
3 tablespoons mayonnaise
2 tablespoons lemon juice
salt and pepper to taste
1 tablespoon canola oil

- Preheat oven to 400°F.

- Mix together all ingredients except for the canola oil and tilapia fillets.

- Pour the oil into a medium baking pan, and place the tilapia fillets on top of the oil.

- Bake for 10 minutes uncovered, then pour sauce over and continue baking until fish is cooked through (around 10 more minutes).

CREAMY CILANTRO SALMON

My family likes to eat salmon for Friday night dinner on Shabbat because it is light and healthy, yet delicious and special. I'm always making up my own recipes based on ingredients I have in the fridge, and this is one of those winning recipes that I discovered when playing around in the kitchen. Enjoy!

INGREDIENTS

6-1 inch wide pieces of salmon fillet
½ cup mayonnaise
½ cup sour cream
3 teaspoons lemon juice
2 tablespoons fresh cilantro, chopped
salt to taste

- Mix all ingredients besides the fish together.

- Grill salmon; 5 minutes before it is done spread the sauce over it.

- Serve hot or cold.

Moroccan Nile

Israel is a melting pot of traditions and recipes from all over the world. This is a recipe that my eighty-five-year-old Moroccan neighbor gave to me, and it is one of my favorite fish recipes in the world. Spicy, delicious, ethnic, and simply perfect!

INGREDIENTS

5 nile fish steaks
3 tablespoons olive oil
¼ cup olive oil
½ cup water
2 tomatoes, diced
¾ cup lemon juice
1 red pepper, sliced
5 cloves garlic, chopped
4 tablespoons paprika
½ tablespoon cumin
salt
1 bushel of fresh cilantro

- Before turning on the flame of the stove: In a big pot put in 3 tablespoons olive oil, tomatoes, fish steaks, lemon juice, salt, sliced red pepper, and garlic.

- Mix dressing and pour over food in pot: ¼ cup olive oil, water, paprika, cumin, and salt.

- Top off with a big bushel of fresh cilantro.

- Turn on stove flame to medium and cook covered for 50 minutes.

Salmon with Spinach Cream Sauce

This spinach cream sauce is perfect for salmon and leftovers taste delicious with pasta, rice, or alone. This creamy sauced fish tastes so lovely that no one will ever believe that it is healthy too!

INGREDIENTS

6-1 inch wide pieces of salmon fillet
½ package frozen chopped spinach, thawed and drained
3 cloves garlic, crushed
½ cup sour cream
1 cup creamer
salt and pepper to taste

- Preheat oven to 400°F.

- Mix all ingredients together and pour over the salmon, in a medium baking dish.

- Bake covered for 20 minutes, baste the salmon in the sauce, then continue baking uncovered until salmon is cooked through (around another 10 minutes).

spice crusted salmon

Spice Crusted Salmon

This salmon is so easy to prepare and utterly delicious. It is a light yet filling main course that I make often for Friday night dinner on Shabbat with some roasted vegetables and rice. The good thing about this recipe is that you already have all of the ingredients in the house! Feel free to substitute bread/cornflake crumbs for Panko.

Ingredients

6-2 inch wide pieces of salmon fillet
juice from one lemon
2 tablespoons olive oil
1 teaspoon sweet paprika
1 teaspoon garlic powder
½ teaspoon ginger powder
1 teaspoon dried dill
salt and pepper to taste
1 cup Japanese bread crumbs (Panko) or bread/cornflake crumbs

- Preheat the oven to 375°F.

- Place the salmon in a greased medium baking dish.

- Cover the salmon in lemon juice and olive oil.

- Sprinkle all of the seasonings over the salmon, and top with Japanese bread crumbs.

- Bake covered for 20 minutes, uncovered for 5 (until the salmon is cooked through).

TERIYAKI SALMON

This recipe is a traditional Eckstein recipe that my mother, my two sisters, and I all make at least once a week. Our kids all call it 'Bubby's candy salmon' referring to my mother that made up this delicious recipe. This salmon is the perfect mixture of sweet and salty, and tastes truly divine!

INGREDIENTS

6-2 inch wide pieces of salmon fillet
¼ cup soy sauce
¼ cup brown sugar
2 tablespoons water
¼ cup lemon juice
salt to taste
¼ teaspoon ginger powder
1 tablespoon canola oil

- Preheat oven to 400°F.

- Mix together all ingredients, except salmon, and pour the sauce over salmon in a medium sized greased baking dish.

- Let it marinate, if possible, for at least 30 minutes.

- Bake uncovered for 15 minutes (or until the salmon is cooked through), baste the salmon every 10 minutes in the sauce .

If you'd like to grill salmon instead: Pour the sauce over salmon, let it marinate if possible, then grill for 20 minutes (or until the salmon is cooked through).

Negligent hands cause poverty but diligent hands enrich

Proverbs 10:4

We all have something special and productive to give the world. Each individual has been provided by God with the exact tools we need in this lifetime. For some people these tools are financial and for others it is simply a positive outlook on life that they can share with others. What are the tools that you possess which have the ability to enrich? Our responsibility is to share what we have with others and in turn, others will share with us. Teachers, doctors, lawyers, Rabbis, priests, and friends are all sharing their strength to better the world. Become aware of your strengths, recognize, and appreciate them. Then, share your wisdom with others, and leave your heart open to learn from other people as well. Only through unity and harmony is this world complete.

My fruit is better than gold and produce better then silver. I walk in the way of righteousness and justice

Proverbs 8:19

We learn from this verse that there is a connection between eating consciously and acting righteously. Try to appreciate where your food came from and give thanks for the energy and life that it provides you with. Envision the fruits and vegetables starting off as a little seed, and the journey that they went through until they landed in your kitchen. Each fruit and vegetable that we eat were ultimately grown and put in the world, exclusively for us. When you look at the world through conscious eyes and are thankful for the little things that many people take for granted, it enables you to act in a righteous and just way.

SOUP

THOSE WHO LOVE ME I LOVE
PROVERBS 8:17

We are all influenced by our surroundings and have our own unique perception of the type of people we are able to love. Although it is rational that we are drawn to people with similar strengths, values, and personality, we should strive not to close ourselves off to others. Drop the misconceptions of who is worthy to love and open up your heart to the world. When someone opens up to love you, treat them with respect and kindness. Use gentle words instead of judgment. When hesitation or judgment creeps in, find three positive strengths in the person you are having a hard time relating to and focus on those things. Recognize how everyone has positive attributes that you can connect to, learn from, and love.

CREAM OF CORN SOUP

Corn is sweet, healthy, and delicious. Growing up in Chicago, we ate a lot of corn. This soup is so tasty and reminds me of my childhood in Midwest America.

INGREDIENTS

1 onion, chopped
2 cloves garlic, chopped
2 tablespoons canola oil
2 medium potatoes, chopped
2 celery stalks, diced
2 tablespoons butter
7 cups water
¼ cup fresh parsley
1 can corn
2 tablespoons cream cheese
salt

- In a medium size pot, heat oil.

- Add onion and garlic and mix over low flame until onion is cooked and clear.

- Add potatoes, celery, butter, and wait for the butter to melt.

- Cover all of the vegetables with water; boil.

- Add 1 tablespoon onion soup mix, fresh parsley, and salt.

- Simmer covered 20 minutes then add corn.

- Blend everything together with an immersion blender.

- Add 2 tablespoon cream cheese and reboil.

CREAM OF ZUCCHINI SOUP

This creamy soup is so tasty that no one believes it is actually healthy! I always have zucchinis in my fridge, so when my children come home on a cold day and say that they want some hot soup, I'm always prepared for this recipe. They never complain when I serve it for dinner!

INGREDIENTS

1 onion, chopped
2 cloves garlic, chopped
2 tablespoons canola oil
2 medium potatoes, chopped
3 zucchinis, diced
2 celery stalks, diced
2 tablespoons butter
7 cups water
1 tablespoon onion soup mix
¼ cup fresh parsley
½ teaspoon salt
2 tablespoons cream cheese

- In medium or large pot, heat oil.

- Sauté onion and garlic until onion is cooked and clear.

- Add potatoes, zucchinis, celery, and butter, and wait for the butter to melt.

- Cover with water (around 7 cups); boil.

- Add onion soup mix, fresh parsley, and salt.

- Simmer covered 20 minutes.

- Blend everything together with immersion blender.

- Add 2 tablespoon cream cheese and reboil.

DO NOT WITHHOLD GOOD FROM ONE WHO DESERVES IT

PROVERBS 3:27

We hold grudges based on past experiences that were emotionally harmful and we let those negative feelings influence our future actions. Actions or words that offend us or make us angry are often simply misunderstandings. When someone does or says something that hurts you, try to think about their intentions; were they intentionally trying to cause you harm and pain? Were they personally going through a difficult time and simply took it out on you? Communication is the best path to healing, so use your words to tell the person how they hurt you – you might be surprised to find out that they weren't even aware of your injured feelings! The best present you can give to yourself, is the gift of forgiveness.

DELICIOUS ORANGE SOUP

When my eldest daughter was a baby, her nanny in Jerusalem would make her this special soup and my precious baby would eat at least two full bowls of it. Seven years later, all three of my kid's favorite soup is 'Shuvi's Orange Soup' and I have perfected the recipe for them. This soup is hearty, delicious, and naturally sweet.

INGREDIENTS

2 tablespoons canola oil
1 onion
2 zucchinis, chopped
3 sweet potatoes, sliced
3 carrots, chopped
½ squash, squared
1 potato, sliced
1 tablespoon chicken soup mix
salt and pepper to taste

- In a large pot, sauté onions and zucchini in heated oil until onions are clear.

- Add the rest of the vegetables and fill with water to cover around three inches above the vegetables.

- Turn the stove on high and add the spices.

- Once the soup is boiling, cover and lower the flame.

- Let the soup cook for around 30 minutes, or until all of the vegetables are soft.

- Use a hand blender to blend the soup and make it creamy.

Hearty Vegetable Barley

I used to always go to restaurants to get vegetable barley soup, until I realized how easy it is to make. This soup is so healthy and includes tons of vegetables, yet it is so delicious that everyone enjoys eating it. On cold winter nights, there are few things better than this special soup!

Ingredients

1 onion, chopped
4 cloves garlic, chopped
2 tablespoons canola oil
10 cherry tomatoes, halved
1 yellow zucchini, sliced
1 green zucchini, sliced
2 carrots, chopped
1 sweet potato, sliced
2 celery stalks, chopped

½ cup cabbage (purple or white), chopped
¾ cup barley
12 cups water
4 tablespoons soy sauce
⅛ teaspoon black pepper
½ teaspoon dried parsley
1 teaspoon dried basil
¼ cup tomato paste

- Heat oil in large pot.

- Sauté onion and garlic until onion is cooked and clear.

- Add cherry tomatoes, yellow zucchini, green zucchini, carrot, sweet potato, celery, and cabbage. Sauté for 5 minutes.

- Add barley and 12 cups of water; boil for 5 minutes.

- Simmer and add soy sauce, black pepper, dried parsley, dried basil, tomato paste, and salt.

- Simmer covered for 40 minutes.

Lentil, Split Pea, & Sweet Potato Soup

This delicious soup is so filling that we often eat it for dinner. The health benefits are endless and best of all, it tastes like it was made in a restaurant. Easy and quick to prepare, this soup is always a complete hit for my family and any guests we have over. My kids love to put soup nuts inside the soup before they eat it, to give it a yummy crunch.

INGREDIENTS

2 tablespoons canola oil
1 onion, chopped
4 cloves garlic, chopped
2 sweet potatoes, cubed
½ cup brown lentils
½ cup yellow split peas
½ cup green split peas
water
1 tablespoon cumin
salt and pepper

- Heat up oil in medium pot.

- Sauté onion and garlic, until onion is clear and cooked.

- Add sweet potatoes, lentils, yellow split peas, and green split peas.

- Fill water to three inches above the mixture.

- Boil for 45 minutes, adding more water as necessary.

- Add cumin, as well as salt and pepper to taste .

- Blend with hand blender (optional).

HAPPY IS THE MAN WHO FINDS WISDOM, THE MAN WHO ATTAINS UNDERSTANDING

PROVERBS 3:13

Much of the physical and emotional anguish that is rampant in our generation is caused by suppression of emotions. We are taught from a young age to swallow our feelings and put on a smile. Our natural instincts in regard to emotions have been lost. If we reclaim the understandings of our hearts, we will acquire wisdom and health. Think about the things that really make you sad and give those things legitimacy, no matter how petty or minute. Then, appreciate the happiness you feel from the small things. Perhaps it is a flower out your window that blooms, a delicious meal, a nice word from your spouse, a kiss from your child, a new pair of shoes. To be aware of your own unique emotions, and allow yourself to cry, laugh, or smile, then you will reclaim your own individual wisdom and completion. When you understand yourself, you can understand the world around you.

Tomato Bisque

I have always loved tomato bisque soup at restaurants, yet after trying dozens of recipes at home that were simply not perfect I decided to make my own recipe. Dozens of trials later, this is the tomato bisque recipe that my family and I like best, and it also happens to be quick and easy. Especially with soup, it's good to get creative!

Ingredients

    2 tablespoons canola oil
    30 cherry tomatoes, uncut, *or* 6 big tomatoes, diced
    1 can crushed tomatoes
    2 onions
    2 cups milk
    1 can coconut liquid *or* 2 cups dairy creamer
    2 cup water
    ½ teaspoon salt

- In a medium sized soup pot, heat oil.

- Sauté chopped onions and garlic in oil until onions are cooked and clear.

- Add cherry tomatoes (uncut) and a can of crushed tomatoes and let simmer for 5 minutes on a medium flame.

- Add milk, coconut milk *or* two cups of sweet dairy creamer, water, and salt; boil.

- Blend and serve!

MOMMA'S CAULIFLOWER SOUP

Just a few blocks away from my house in northern Israel are huge fields where farmers grow cauliflower, so my local community always has cauliflower in abundance. This creamy and savory soup is so delicious and bursting with flavor, yet takes just four ingredients and a few minutes to prepare.

INGREDIENTS

water
1 head cauliflower, cut in to pieces
1 medium to large Idaho potato, peeled and cubed
½ cup chicken soup mix
2 cups of mozzarella or cheddar cheese, shredded

- Place cut cauliflower into a large pot, then fill the pot with water.

- Add potato and chicken soup mix.

- Bring to boil, cover, and simmer for 20 minutes.

- Using an immersion blender, blend potato and most of cauliflower, leaving over some florets for garnish.

- Place a pinch of shredded cheddar or mozzarella cheese in each individual bowl immediately before serving.

*traditional
chicken soup*

TRADITIONAL CHICKEN SOUP

Chicken soup is a traditional dish in Jewish culture and it also happens to hold plenty of health benefits for when you are sick with a cold or the flu. Every Friday night when I was growing up at my mother's house, she would make this chicken soup which would warm my body and soul. I feel blessed that today I get to pass on this tradition to my children!

INGREDIENTS

1 chicken, cut into 8 pieces
2 tablespoons canola oil
2 carrots, chopped
1 big onion, sliced
3 celery stalks, sliced
1 zucchini, chopped
1 tablespoon chicken soup mix
salt and pepper
fresh dill to taste

- In a large pot, heat oil.

- Add onions, celery, zucchini, and carrots; sauté for 5 minutes, stirring often.

- Add chicken and water that covers three inches above the chicken.

- Add chicken soup mix; salt and pepper to taste.

- Bring to boil and then simmer for 35 minutes, adding water as needed.

- Garnish with fresh dill.

Kindnesss and truth don't let leave you, write them on your heart.

Proverbs 3:3

We all have values that we cherish so much, which we try to never waiver from. Yet during periods of stress and pressure those values often take the backseat. Become aware of the attributes that you want to encompass, and write them on your heart. If lying appalls you, take a vow to yourself to always tell the truth. If kindness entices you, tattoo it on your soul to follow you wherever you go. Write these values on your heart, and as long as your heart is beating, you will keep those values alive.

IF WE HAD TWO HEARTS LIKE
WE HAVE TWO ARMS AND TWO LEGS,
THEN ONE HEART COULD BE USED
FOR LOVE AND THE OTHER ONE FOR
HATE. SINCE I HAVE BUT ONE HEART,
THEN I DON'T HAVE THE LUXURY
OF HATING ANYONE.

—RABBI SHLOMO CARLEBACH—